Introduction

The poems in this book are all about courage and empowerment. One way to empower someone is to give them the courage to be confident, strong and free. Empowerment is something you can help to give to others and it is also a precious gift you can give to yourself.

But how can these things be in a poem? If you turned the page upside down, would courage and empowerment spill out? What would that look like? Perhaps like a celebration of your culture and heritage, or the moment you find your voice. Maybe it would look like learning to live with imperfection, being true to yourself or discovering your potential.

These poems are little parcels of empowerment that the poets are giving specially to you. They are gifts that you can keep and pass along. Remember, courage grows when shared!

LITTLE TIGER

LONDON

Contents

- 6   Song for Exploding Stars – *Cecilia Knapp*
- 8   My Sari – *Debjani Chatterjee*
- 10   I Did It – *Valerie Bloom*
- 12   The Cancan – *Mandy Coe*
- 13   Courage – *Naomi Shihab Nye*
- 14   Your Epic Self – *Kate Wakeling*
- 16   Unfurling People – *Elizabeth Acevedo*
- 18   Afro Hair Haiku – *Victoria Adukwei Bulley*
- 20   Dislexsic Poim – *Joe Cook*
- 22   A Talkin'-To – *Jason Reynolds*
- 24   Mistakes – *Nikita Gill*
- 26   You're Never Too… – *Laura Mucha*
- 28   You Can Do It Right Now – *Janet Wong*
- 30   Getting Started – *Nikki Grimes*
- 32   Instructions on Listening to the Trees – *Mahogany L. Browne*
- 34   You See? – *Matt Goodfellow*
- 35   Mother's Eyes – *Sophia Thakur*
- 36   Being True to Yourself – *Rachel Plummer*
- 38   To Be a Man – *Jay Hulme*
- 40   My Heart Soars – *Chief Dan George*
- 42   Biographies
- 45   Copyright and Acknowledgements

Song for Exploding Stars

You are an exploding star. Sparks into dark blue.

You are a firework. You are a solar system and the telescope
to watch the planets through.

You are the smell of spring. You are a whole row of sunflowers,
standing tall. You are the way the moon dips into water
and the echo of a bird's call.

You are flames. You are the way the fireflies glow.
You are thunderstorms and hilltops, all the colours of the rainbow.

You are waves crashing on a shore, you can be hurricanes.
You are ancient rivers and waterfalls. You are the gentle summer rain.

You are the perfect satsuma. You are the electric fizz of tangy sweets.
You are a thick slice of rich cake. You are a drink
of cold water in the heat.

You are the cheer when a goal is scored, when a ball makes a net shake.
You are an aeroplane soaring through the air.
You are a boat sailing on a lake.

You are the chorus of a song, the bass line and the beat.
You are clapping hands and shouts of joy.
You are the spotlight's heat.

You are a mathematic equation. You are whole libraries stacked tall.
You are stories and poems and myths and plays, the wonder of it all.

You are the vibrant city. You are all the pennies in the fountain.
You're skyscrapers and bridges, roads
that lead to the top of a mountain.

You are all the good things. Though it can be easy to forget,
fill up rooms with your brilliance, your voice
and don't you ever let

anyone tell you you're anything less than brilliant and bright.
You are the future, you are hope.
You are the sun bursting through the night.

And though there might be those in life who tell you that you're not,
you hold so much greatness in your palm, so don't you ever stop.

Cecilia Knapp

My Sari

Saris hang on the washing line:
a rainbow in our neighbourhood.
This little orange one is mine,
it has a mango leaf design.
I wear it as a Rani would.
It wraps around me like sunshine,
it ripples silky down my spine,
and I stand tall and feel so good.

Debjani Chatterjee

I Did It

They said I shouldn't do it
'Cause I was just a child,
They said I couldn't do it,
But I just quietly smiled.
It's too long a ride, they said,
And you look so unfit.
But I didn't listen to them,
I got on my bike and did it.

You're just a girl, they said,
And it's very plain to see
That girls are not built for such things
(It wasn't plain to me).
It's unheard of! It's preposterous!
Unthinkable! Quite absurd!
But I went and did it anyway,
And they didn't say a word.

They said, What! A physician?
That's not a job for you.
Why not be a secretary?
That's something you could do.
No one from your neighbourhood
Has completed a degree,
So you can't be a doctor!
Oh no? Just wait and see!

Valerie Bloom

The Cancan

When I dance
my blood runs like a river can,
my feet fly like the birds can,
my heart beats like a drum can.
Because when I dance I can,
can do anything
when I dance.

Flying over rooftops
I see my town below me
where everybody knows me,
where all my problems throw me,
where heavy feet can slow me.
But nobody can, can stop me
when I dance.

My blood runs a race.
My feet fly in space.
My heart beats the pace.
Because when I dance I can,
can do anything
when I dance.

Mandy Coe

Courage

A word must travel through
a tongue and teeth and wide air
to get there.
A word has tough skin.

To be let in,
a word must slide and sneak
and spin into the tunnel of the ear.
What's to fear?
Everything.
But a word
is brave.

Naomi Shihab Nye

Your Epic Self

Ocean deep,
quick as a comet,
your epic self is a force beyond.

You can open any lock,
you can scale any cliff,
you can sniff out a lie from a mile off.

I once saw you switch
on every lightbulb in town
with just your smile.

Your ideas are a fistful of gold pieces,
your words are strong as salt.

You can keep a secret quieter than clouds
but when you see a wrong not put right,
oh there's no sound
mightier than your tiger roar.

And sure,
your epic self doesn't surface every day.

No one's does.

But know it's there,
tucked deep,
ready and waiting.

Sure as an anchor,
bright as the moon,
your epic self is a force beyond.

Kate Wakeling

Unfurling People

People leave their homes
even when they love their homes
because people are like flowers:
and sometimes, the places where we live
do not have enough to water us all,
or they have enough sunlight,
but it's being used to scorch us;
or the soil is fertile, but those who tend it
want to pluck us straight out
before we've grown to our full potential.
And so, immigration is like tucking your roots
carefully into yourself
and repotting in a different land.

Immigration is an attempt to
bloom and blossom
and brighten a new place
with the colors and scents
you've brought with you.
It is an attempt to remember
where you are from, and the
place that made you,
and also unfurl to the possibilities
of the new place you call home.

Immigration is learning to stretch
into a bridge,
backward and forward,
one limb in each place,
learning to hold tight to traditions
and customs and names and memories in one hand,
and with the other hand let go and lean in
to a place you hope will see you
for all the beauty that you bring.

Elizabeth Acevedo

Afro Hair Haiku

My hair shrinks when wet,
like pine cones in the autumn
waiting for their time.

Here's one thing I love:
to curl it round my fingers
and watch it bounce back.

Sometimes I wear braids.
Other times I wear cornrows.
Any style looks good.

I used to harm it,
force it down, flat and lifeless –
a ghost of itself.

Now I let it grow
the way it wants to grow:
confident again.

Victoria Adukwei Bulley

Dislexsic Poim

I represent the kid whose struggle is unseen
Who can't fit into life's routine
Whose heart races when asked to read out loud
Whose silver lining is just thunder clouds
Who chews up knowledge and lets wisdom digest
But whose belly is empty when it comes to a test
Who's got grades to gain and points to score
But can't get a hand on this double-edged sword
Who can't follow the movement
Thinks there's no room for improvement
And I don't feel bad for nodding off in class
Like Gandalf was marking my work – you shall not pass
An underachiever daydreamer
Every day brainteaser
Words don't escape me, they help me to escape

So don't try to measure my intelligence
It's got no colour, size, weight or shape
There they're their – they're all the same
Scrabble is the devil's game
Write your own rules
With grammatical errors and spelling mistakes
'Cause you're a champion, you got what it takes
You're greater than a grade, you're bigger than an IQ
The only one who can build and destroy those barriers is you
So when you feel the weight and the pressure
Remember that's how diamonds are made in nature
It's not a learning difficulty
We just learn differently

Joe Cook

A Talkin'-To

I could tell you all the bad things,
all the bad things that cut and scare
and howl and growl and gnash and
bear teeth, bright and sharp that
glint in the moonlight.

I could tell you all that's frightening,
all that's frightening and lurking
and looming and hiding in the brush,
razor-hair pricked up on the back
of something too sly to see.

I could tell you about all the loud things,
all the loud things that scream
and shriek and shred our ability to hear
each other, the beasts behind screens,
scrolling banners of bully-banter.

I could tell you all the things,
all the things that are trying to tell you
about you, about how you should run,
and how you should run,
and how you should run,
but I'm about you above all things,
above all things, so I'd rather tell you
one thing and one thing only:

everything bad and frightening and loud
will always hide when you hold your head up,
will always hide when you hold your heart out,
will always sing a shrinking song
when you fly.

Jason Reynolds

Mistakes

So many of the trees and the rivers we love
came to be because
Nature made a mistake.

It planted trees where none lived before,
It made a river run through a forest
where no river was ever there before.

And this is how some of the strangest places
are now home to the most beautiful trees
and we have forest rivers that give clear water

to deer and wolves
and robins and sparrows
and grasshoppers and even the bees.

The best thing about you
is that you too will make mistakes.
And you will learn from them

to become a better version of you.
You do not need to be ashamed
of the things you did wrong when learning.

You just need to do what nature did.
Grow a beautiful forest and rivers inside yourself
where the mistakes once lived

all because you were brave enough
to grow in all the places
no one ever thought you could.

Nikita Gill

You're Never Too...

You're never too poor to give away kindness,
you're never too rich to feel sadness or fear,
you're never too quiet to make others listen,
you're never too loud to stop and to hear.

You're never too guilty to ask for forgiveness,
you're never too flawless to need help to cope,
you're never too big to feel ever-so-tiny,
you're never too little to give someone hope.

You're never too foolish to try to be wiser,
you're never too smart to need time to heal,
you're never too this or too that to make changes,
you're never too young to say how you feel.

Laura Mucha

You Can Do It Right Now

You can shout at a march.
You can quietly pray.
You can read the news
and share it today.
You can send the mayor
of your town a note.
You can make a sign
that tells people to vote.
You can talk to your family.
You can listen to friends.

There are different ways
to reach the same ends,
to fight injustice,
to show that you care.

You can do it right now,
from anywhere.

Janet Wong

Getting Started

Say "fly,"
and I go back to the
first daydream
that saved me.
I remember
there were screams,
a plate crashing
to the kitchen floor,
and angry words
ripping the air.
I pulled the pillow
over my head,
dove deeper under the covers.
Still, I could hear the awful sound
of their raised voices.
"Lalalalalala," I said aloud.
Still, I could hear them.
If only I could fly, I thought.
*If I could fly, fly, fly away,
I'd go to the window,
step out on the ledge,
spread my wings and fly way
high above the city,
higher than the clouds.
I'd fly straight to Virginia,
fly to Great-Grandma's house.*

I'd land on the porch,
hop on her swing,
and listen to her hum,
hum, humming to me.
And just then,
I could almost hear
Great-Grandma's hum,
could almost feel the gentle sway
of the porch swing.
And for a few moments,
I forgot
my parents fighting.
The word *fly*
had set me free,
and I wondered,
*Are there other words
that can carry me away?*

Nikki Grimes

Instructions on Listening to the Trees

When you are part of a community
You have to think about others

Think about the sun
And how it smiles sweet authority
Think about the ecosystem
And how the leaves dress the tree trunks
Surviving from the kindness of the sun
Yes, the sun and trees have a community all their own

And aren't we part of their community, too?
Benefiting from the oxygen and water, it creates new life
The water is alive in its gift giving
Think of how it feeds the roots

Like any true community
We must nourish and care for one another
If we are to grow

So I listen to the trees when the wind dances near
And I listen to the neighbor's dog singing to the moon
The moon is high because of the water
How amazing!

And this is when I remember home
the way my friends ring the doorbell to come outside and play
the way a car slows down when a ball rolls in its way
the way we make jokes about the TV show and share our fears
the way we look up sadly when the streetlights come on

We all are part of someone else's journey
That's the way communities are built
Each root sprawling toward the edge of an infinite smile

Mahogany L. Browne

You See?

kind words stick to me
like pollen to the knee of a bee
or should that be its thigh
anyhow I
don't mind
but I do care about kind
(and hope you agree)
because now I find
I'm a kind word collector
each one's my protector
yes
kindness
is nectar
to me

Matt Goodfellow

Mother's Eyes

If only for a moment
I could borrow my mother's eyes
and see myself as she does.
Love myself as she does
and believe in myself with the same
certainty that she does...
as if all I can do is win.

I guess after carrying me for nine months
she is well trained in the faith
that whenever there is cause to push,
only in complete surrender to bravery
can I deliver
exactly what I was born to do...

Born to be
my mother's faith in me.

Sophia Thakur

Being True to Yourself

In the woods, a tree.
By the river, a beech tree.
With exposed roots, a tall beech tree.

I wish I could be so fully myself
as this tree is fully a tall beech tree.
I wish I could plant myself
so sturdy in the soil.

The tree is its own shape.
Twisted and stooped, this tree
is the shape of a beech tree.

I wish I could be so fully my own shape.
I wish I could rest easy
on my own roots.
I wish that when I laughed,
the mast* of my old self would fall
and crunch underfoot all winter.

*mast – the fruit of a beech tree

By the stone beach, a beech tree.

The tree asks no permission.
The beech tree makes no apologies.
The tall beech tree.

It thinks in leaves and speaks
in the movement of the leaves
and says

I will take space from the air.
I will take up space in the woods.
I will open my arms wide.
I will lose all I have and regain it.
I will be nothing but myself.

I am. I will grow.

Rachel Plummer

To Be a Man

My grandad sat me down one day
and said: to be a man
there is one thing that you must do,
and do it best you can.

Manhood isn't something
that's awarded on your turn.
Manhood isn't something
that's made difficult to earn.

Manhood isn't made at all,
but grows, just like a tree,
bursting up inside yourself,
uncurling from a seed.

It's not about your clothes,
and it's not about your figure,
it's not about lifting weights
to build your muscles bigger.

It's not about holding doors,
boys, that's just polite;
it's not about ignoring fears
that keep you up at night.

It's not about the ladies,
and it's not about the lads.
It's not about the things you want
or the things you have.

You don't have to be 'manly'
or anything but you.
A man is simply who you are,
not what you have to prove.

The only thing to do is this:
live boldly; live your life;
for if you're true to who you are,
you're doing manhood right.

Jay Hulme

My Heart Soars

The beauty of the trees,
the softness of the air,
the fragrance of the grass,
speaks to me.

The summit of the mountain,
the thunder of the sky,
the rhythm of the sea,
speaks to me.

The faintness of the stars,
the freshness of the morning,
the dew drop on the flower,
speaks to me.

The strength of fire,
the taste of salmon,
the trail of the sun,
And the life that never goes away,
They speak to me.

And my heart soars.

Chief Dan George

Biographies

Cecilia Knapp

Cecilia Knapp is a poet, playwright, novelist and the lead tutor for the Roundhouse's prestigious poetry collective. She was the 2020-2021 Young People's Laureate for London and the resident poet at Great Ormond Street Hospital. Her debut novel, *Little Boxes*, and debut poetry collection, *Peach Pig*, were published in 2022.

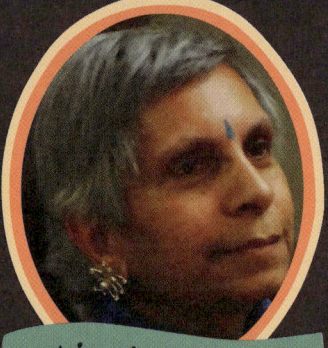
Debjani Chatterjee

Debjani Chatterjee is an Indian-born poet who has written and edited over 70 books, including plays and retellings of traditional tales for children. She is a Fellow of the Royal Society of Literature and Associate Fellow of the Royal Literary Fund. In 2008 she received an MBE.

Valerie Bloom

Winner of the 2022 CLiPPA, Valerie Bloom has written and edited many highly acclaimed children's poetry books; her writing is heavily influenced by her Jamaican background. She has performed widely and appeared on radio and TV. She received an MBE for services to poetry in 2007.

Mandy Coe

An award-winning author of eight books, Mandy Coe writes poetry for adults and children. She works in education and on literacy projects through residencies, workshops and readings.

Naomi Shihab Nye

Palestinian-American poet Naomi Shihab Nye has written books for adults and children, including *Sitti's Secrets* and *Habibi* which both won the Jane Addams Children's Book Award. She was the 2019-2022 Poetry Foundation's Young People's Poet Laureate and received the Ivan Sandrof Lifetime Achievement Award from the National Book Critics Circle in 2020.

Kate Wakeling

Kate Wakeling grew up in Yorkshire and Birmingham. Her first collection of poems for children, *Moon Juice*, won the 2017 CLiPPA and her second collection, *Cloud Soup*, was a book of the month in the *Guardian* and *The Scotsman*.

Photo credit: Sophie Davidson

Elizabeth Acevedo

Elizabeth Acevedo is the bestselling and award-winning author of *The Poet X* and *With the Fire on High*. She holds an MFA in Creative Writing and is a National Poetry Slam Champion. Elizabeth resides in Washington, DC.

Victoria Adukwei Bulley

Victoria Adukwei Bulley is a poet, writer and artist. An alumna of the Barbican Young Poets, her work has appeared widely in publications. Her debut poetry collection, *Quiet*, was published by Faber & Faber in 2022.

Joe Cook is a spoken word artist and musician from Birmingham, UK. He facilitates poetry/rap music and drumming workshops across the Midlands. Joe worked with BBC Arts to release a video of 'How To Be a Poet With Dyslexia'.

Photo credit: Chris Neophyto

Jason Reynolds is a #1 *New York Times* bestselling author and winner of the 2021 CILIP Carnegie Medal. He is also a Newbery Award Honoree, a Printz Award Honoree, a two-time National Book Award finalist, and was the 2020–2022 US National Ambassador for Young People's Literature. His many books include *All American Boys*, the *RUN* series, *Look Both Ways*, *Stamped* and *Long Way Down*.

Nikita Gill is an Irish-Indian poet who has 700,000 Instagram followers worldwide. She has been shortlisted for a CLiPPA and the Goodreads Choice Award, longlisted for the Jhalak Children's and YA Prize and was nominated for a Carnegie in 2023. Gill has written seven poetry collections, a verse novel and a book of fables.

Laura Mucha is an ex-lawyer turned award-winning poet and author. Her writing has been featured on TV, radio and public transport, as well as in hospitals, hospices, prisons, books, magazines and newspapers around the world. For more info, visit lauramucha.com

Photo credit: David Yeo

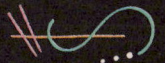

Janet Wong is an American poet and children's book author of over 30 titles. She is the co-publisher of Pomelo Books and the winner of the 2021 NCTE Award for Excellence in Poetry for Children, a prestigious lifetime achievement award.

Photo credit: Emily Vardell

New York Times bestselling author Nikki Grimes is the recipient of the 2020 ALAN Award for outstanding contributions to young adult literature, and the 2017 Children's Literature Legacy Award among other prestigious awards for her distinguished body of children's books.

Mahogany L. Browne is a writer, organiser and educator based in Brooklyn. She is the author of *Woke: A Young Poet's Call to Justice* and *Black Girl Magic* among others. Mahogany is the founder of the diverse literature initiative Woke Baby Book Fair.

Matt Goodfellow is a poet. When he's not at home writing, he spends most of his time travelling around the UK and beyond visiting schools, libraries and festivals, performing and helping people write their own poems.

Sophia Thakur

Sophia Thakur's debut poetry collection *Somebody Give This Heart a Pen* has inspired varied audiences across the world from the Glastonbury stage to countless mainstream TV and radio segments. Her latest book *Superheroes* went straight to the bestseller list after launching.

Photo credit: Chantal Azari

Rachel Plummer

Rachel Plummer is a poet based in Edinburgh. They were a Troubadour International Poetry Prize winner in 2014. Their debut children's poetry collection, *Wain*, is based around LGBT retellings of traditional Scottish myths.

Jay Hulme

Jay Hulme is an award-winning transgender performance poet, speaker and educator. Jay teaches in schools and consults with groups on the importance of diversity and transgender inclusion in literature and the media.

Chief Dan George

Chief Dan George was an actor, musician, poet and author. He was chief of the Tsleil-Waututh Nation, a Coast Salish band located in the southeast area of the District of North Vancouver, British Columbia, Canada.

Annalise Barber

A resident of Columbus, Ohio, Annalise Barber illustrates for children and those who are young at heart. She experiments with sinuous shapes, playful narratives and watercolour media. With a paintbrush in her hand, Annalise illustrates to inspire and empower children.

Mariana Roldán

Mariana Roldán is an illustrator based in Mexico. She loves to dance and draw. These activities are how she expresses the feelings that live inside her and how she shares with others the history of the world we live in.

Masha Manapov

Masha Manapov is an award-winning illustrator, author and image maker. Born in Baku and raised in Tel Aviv, she is currently working from her London-based studio on commissioned projects worldwide.

Nabila Adani

Nabila Adani lives in Jakarta, Indonesia, and enjoys illustrating different world cultures. She briefly worked as a product designer before moving to the United States to study children's book illustration. Now, living back in Jakarta, she enjoys illustrating and telling stories for children worldwide.

Copyright and Acknowledgements

LITTLE TIGER
An imprint of Little Tiger Press Limited
1 Coda Studios, 189 Munster Road, London SW6 6AW
www.littletiger.co.uk
Imported into the EEA by Penguin Random House Ireland,
Morrison Chambers, 32 Nassau Street, Dublin D02 YH68
www.littletigerpress.com
First published in Great Britain 2022 • This edition published 2026
P2-3, 10-11, 18-19, 22-23, 32-33, 35, 46-47 illustrations copyright © Masha Manapov 2022
P12, 16-17, 26-27, 38-39 illustrations copyright © Nabila Adani 2022
P8-9, 20-21, 24-25, 30-31, 36-37 illustrations copyright © Annalise Barber 2022
P6-7, 14-15, 28-29, 40-41 illustrations copyright © Mariana Roldán 2022
Cover copyright © Masha Manapov 2022
'Song for Exploding Stars' written by Cecilia Knapp © Cecilia Knapp 2019,
granted with permission of Lewinsohn Literary Agency.
Thanks to Debjani Chatterjee for permission to use her poem 'My Sari', published in *Masala: Poems from India,
Bangladesh, Pakistan and Sri Lanka* ed. Debjani Chatterjee (Macmillan Children's Books, 2005).
'I Did It' by Valerie Bloom © Valerie Bloom 2022
'The Cancan' written by Mandy Coe from *If You Could See Laughter* (Salt, 2010) © Mandy Coe, 2010.
Reproduced with permission of the Licensor through PLSclear.
Poetry selection titled: 'Courage' from *Everything Comes Next* by Naomi Shihab Nye – Read By: Naomi Shihab Nye, James Patrick Cronin.
Copyright © 2020 by Naomi Shihab Nye. Used by permission of HarperCollins Publishers.
'Your Epic Self' by Kate Wakeling © Kate Wakeling 2022
'Unfurling People' by Elizabeth Acevedo and 'Instructions on Listening to the Trees' by Mahogany L. Browne from *Woke: A Young Poet's Call to
Justice* by Mahogany L. Browne with Elizabeth Acevedo and Olivia Gatwood; illustrated by Theodore Taylor III, foreword by Jason Reynolds.
'Unfurling People' copyright © 2020 by Elizabeth Acevedo. 'Instructions on Listening to the Trees' copyright © 2020 by Mahogany L. Browne.
Reprinted by permission of Roaring Brook Press, a division of Holtzbrinck Publishing Holdings Limited Partnership. All Rights Reserved.
'Afro Hair Haiku' from *Rising Stars* (Otter-Barry Books, 2017) by Victoria Adukwei Bulley
© Victoria Adukwei Bulley 2017. Used by kind permission of the author.
'Dislexsic Poim' by Joe Cook © Joe Cook 2016. Used by kind permission of the author.
'A Talkin'-To' by Jason Reynolds from *We Rise, We Resist, We Raise Our Voices* (Crown Books for Young Readers, 2018),
compiled by Wade Hudson and Cheryl Willis Hudson. Copyright © 2018 by Jason Reynolds.
'Mistakes' by Nikita Gill © Nikita Gill 2022
'You're Never Too...' by Laura Mucha © Laura Mucha 2022
'You Can Do It Right Now' by Janet Wong; poem copyright © 2020 by Janet S. Wong,
found in *Hop to It: Poems to Get You Moving* (Pomelo Books, 2020). Used by kind permission of the author.
'Getting Started' from *Words with Wings* by Nikki Grimes. Text copyright © 2013 by Nikki Grimes. Published by
Wordsong, an imprint of Boyds Mills & Kane, a division of Astra Publishing House. Reprinted by permission.
'You See?' by Matt Goodfellow © Matt Goodfellow 2022
'Mother's Eyes' by Sophia Thakur © Sophia Thakur 2022
'Being True to Yourself' by Rachel Plummer © Rachel Plummer 2022
'To Be a Man' by Jay Hulme © Jay Hulme 2022
'My Heart Soars' by Chief Dan George from *The Best of Chief Dan George*, copyright © 2004 by Hancock House
Publishers Ltd., ISBN 978-0888395443, used with permissions - www.hancockhouse.com
Compilation copyright © Little Tiger Press Limited 2022
A CIP catalogue record for this book is available from the British Library
All rights reserved • Printed in China
ISBN: 978-1-83891-959-7 • CPB/2700/3128/0925
2 4 6 8 10 9 7 5 3 1

This book contains poetry in both British and American English. Though the differences are small, we've chosen to keep all writing in its original dialect. The messages in each poem are for everyone but they are also rooted in the places they were dreamt up and written. We wanted to reflect this.

The Forest Stewardship Council® (FSC®) is a global, not-for-profit organisation dedicated to the promotion of responsible forest management worldwide. FSC® defines standards based on agreed principles for responsible forest stewardship that are supported by environmental, social, and economic stakeholders.

To learn more, visit www.fsc.org